Bachelard Interpreted 1

A Choir Of Whispers

Frank Prem

Wild Arancini Press
2024

Publication Details

Title: A Choir of Whispers: Bachelard Interpreted Book 1

ISBN: 978-1-923166-23-3 (p-bk)
ISBN: 978-1-925963-18-2 (e-bk)

Published by Wild Arancini Press
Copyright © 2024 Frank Prem
All rights reserved:

Cover Concept: Wild Arancini Press
Cover Image AI assistant: Adobe Firefly

Given space, you and I may *be*.

CONTENTS

A Choir Of Whispers

A Choir Of Whispers

Introduction

French scientist and philosopher Gaston Bachelard (1884 - 1962) explored and examined poetics and poetry in great depth over the course of his lifetime, particularly examining the poetics of natural elements, of which he identified the four that are traditionally considered:

Fire
Water
Air
Earth

In addition, however, he (effectively) identified two further elements, or dimensions, for his examination:

Time
Space

The *Bachelard Interpreted* poetry series responds to each of these elements and dimensions, as well as encompassing some of Bachelard's further scientific and literary interests.

A *Choir of Whispers* takes Bachelard's explorations of the poetic possibilities inherent in psychological, emotional, and physical space and interprets the concepts and ideas he described in his seminal work *The Poetics of Space* (1964) into new and interpretive poetry.

This collection explores ideas of confinement and expansion, the concept of space as a location to store memories, feelings and associations. Places in the heart, both locked and open. It considers our lives, from basement to attic and from a lidded shoebox filled with unexpected memories to chest of drawers containing unexpected revelations.

A *Choir of Whispers* follows Bachelard through all the rooms of the mind and lays them out in the accessible format of free-verse story-telling poetry.

Note: A *Choir of Whispers* is one of a series of poetry collections inspired by the work of Gaston Bachelard. References to the Bachelard translations that have been relied on as source materials for this project are listed at the end of this book.

The Poetics of Space

a fine cabinetry

it was the work
of a craftsman

a cabinet maker

the construction
not of the cabinet
but its *drawer*

fine-jointed

a neat alignment
of dovetails
tight-fitted

the wood treated
lovingly
to emphasize natural
highlights

finished
with shine
and a warm glow

concealed
within the grain
a false section
accessible only by
trick
or feel

sized to accommodate
this drawer
was a smooth glider
and responsive

over the years
it had grown
from desk size
to deep filing cabinet

both its compartments
now
so much bigger

and the false place —
the *secret holder* —
resides a long way
down

the inheritance

it was a closet
of sorts
a tiny room-space
for storing things
not
in current use

> *small chests*
> *caskets*
> *biscuit tins*
> *with commemorative pictures*
> *stamped*
> *into the metal of the lid*
>
> *shoe boxes*

one on top of another
stacked only enough
to ensure
there could be no chaos
through slippage

a cascade of colour
with each container
tentatively sealed

held closed from the outside
as though to prevent
a random attempted escape
by the contents

from the floor
to above her full height . . .

stack beside stack
filled the space
cubically

she tentatively grasped
one small chest
and turned the key . . .
raised the lid . . .

and . . .

oh!

the sound

the colour

the sensation
of feet
kicking through
the autumn's leaves

the lacquered box

when he opened the box
he found a small stack
of unsealed —
much handled —
letters

loosely bound
by a knotted string
together with a shivered splinter
of wood

> *the splinter*
> *fit*
> *into a space . . .*
>
> *the bottom of the box*
> *loosened*
>
> *came out . . .*

lying flat on the new bottom
of the box
was a photograph —
discoloured sepia —
together with a shivered splinter
of wood

> *the splinter*
> *fit*
> *into a space . . .*
>
> *the bottom of the box*
> *loosened*
>
> *came out . . .*

lying flat on the new bottom
of the box
was a lock
of golden hair

soft and delicate

bound by a strip
of scarlet ribbon
together
with a shivered splinter
of wood . . .

he looked
a long time
at the wooden splinter

then slowly put the pieces
of the lacquered box —
and their secrets —
back together
the way they had been
before

snail

I am home
in the *here*
I am

I *think* my house
grown
all around me

when I move
my home and I
are only
one
wherever
we go

I grow my home
with spit
from the heart
of my deep
desire

and we are one

we will
be one

until
the day
we die

tap tap

tap tap
the walls
for distant oscillations

peri-peer
the turret
what comes
what is close

stethoscope
my ears
the air is noise

sphyg- my blood
so high
it bursts

me **shaped now**

there is a *me* shaped space
right here
where I stand

there was nothing
before

there will be nothing
when I leave

just a *me* space
that used to be
but . . .

you won't find it
where it *was*

you won't find it
where I *am*

I don't *look* like that
anymore

I am not
shaped
like that anymore

I am a *new*-shaped space
right here
where I stand

and it's a *me* shape
because
here I am

right now

angled all right

she sat down
on the west line

leaned back
against the north post

the light played
across her
to burn her shadow
on the ground

stretched into
the east plane
an elongated
dark spectre

she shaped herself
adjacent
to the night

humming a soft tune —
haunting —
in the still air

sitting
doing nothing
in the streetlamp's angle

feeling
right at home

contemplation in the heart

contemplative spider
absently
draws forth a thread . . .

a little spin
of silk

    cat's whiskers
    jacob's ladder
    witch's broom

    dream catcher

    web

spin
spin

she doesn't think about it
her little mind
is not engaged

she has legs
that know to spin
while she

casts her thoughts
to the wind

spin
spin
spin

every strand
in its place
and she —
resident —
in the heart
of her meditation

half (a perspective)

he lived in the centre
of *full*
and *empty*

a step too far . . .

. . . raf oot pets a

would tilt the line
so he lived
in the middle

on the
half line
of the glass

sometimes the world
seemed no more
than glum

sometimes heady . . .

filled with choice

but always
one small step
would change perspective

and
it all looked right
from where *he* lived
in the heart

drift

turning through the air —
spinning
under sunlight —
the mote
is a colour
that changes
all the time

how long has it been
afloat
in such random seas

better to ask

> *how wide is air*
>
> *how tall*
> *the sky*
>
> *how deep*
> *is time*

turning
through the morning

spinning
out of the light

invisible in shadow
a mote

to a corner
it rides the current
of a random breeze
then settles
awhile
to wait
again

centre-side

I am the centre
from the sidelines

you see me
in a corner

I
see everywhere
and from here
there is nothing
not I

you want me?
come find me
I will see you
before you arrive

from the centre
on the sidelines
I
see everything

pea leaf and river

she set her house
and a sail
on the pod
of a pea
then
rode the current
down

for the sea was south
and her house —
so small —
could bob and bounce
and float
while a spinnaker
embraced the wind

or else she rowed

caught three leaves
that fluttered as they fell
from the sky
into the river
on a common path
towards the end

a raft
made of pea and leaf

a house
and the river road

she remembered the wind
and so she sailed
from the *up*
above
to the down below

to the end
that was waiting

after the dream

it was like . . .

it was like
a cloak

waving just in front of me

moving away

each time I reached
to get hold of it
it moved out of range
again

I wanted it
so badly . . .

to hold it
to wear it

to *be* it

can you understand
it was *me*

of me

the me that I could become

something that I already was
but had never seen in myself
before

if only I could catch it . . .

look at it

understand it

but the closer I came
the more
it shimmered into blur

and when I caught
a small piece
in the fist of my hand . . .

it became dust
dull sprinkles
without any spark

it was *not-me*
just a poor
poor
delusion

to you and now a moment

I saw you
in a moment —
just once —
but
that glance
endured

I recall you —
in a moment
blurred
around the edges —
taking up the space
that is
another moment

I give my moments
to the you
that I recall

I give my moments
now and now and now and now . . .

to you

here
and in the moment

from the tower

from where he stood
the world —
as vast as it is —
was a small one

the movement below . . .

a scurry of insects
wearing shadow shades
and black

so far below

> *I*
> *yes I*
> *am the mighty*

he contemplated
the distance down

the distance wide

the distance far
to the tiny-ness
of events on the horizon

shapes
like a topiary of trees
done bonsai

shapes
like an assembly
of children's
building blocks
playthings

> *oh yes it is I*
> *who is mighty here*
> *the one*
> *who stands so high*

truly
it is me

no one is higher
no one is bigger
no one
nearer
to the grace of god

only heaven
is above and it is I
standing in the place between

from where he stood
the world around
seemed
so very small

hearing

she spoke into the silence

the sound
swept up and taken

nothing
where her voice
had been

but
she heard
the passing of a moment

the soft hiss
of a rush
of seconds

the slow wave of *then*
crashing down upon the sands
of *now*

and almost . . .

almost
she made to speak
again

but her voice
could not be located

had passed into
the soundless void

which pressed —
impressed —
a susurrus
inside

inside her
until she heard

constructing me

I
am not really me
you know

it's strange
but
I carry a picture

see there
that is who
I am supposed to be

that is how
I should appear
to you

I'm not really me
the way you see me

no
that
is just your construct

and I have my own
me construct
that I rely upon
to get me through
each thought of mine
and every action

to keep me
assembled well enough
that I can share an image
with you

so you
can make your construct
approximate
to the *really me*
you know

the story

and with the stroke
of a pen
I raise myself —
elevated —
into the god
of everything
I write . . .

I pour
molten gold
and shape it
ha!
these are *my* words
it is *I*
in my guise
of creator

ha! nothing
until I press my pen
to the white

my will
is *all*

let me tell you
a story . . .

it is
my story

I made it
emerge
from the deep
of my mind

ha!
I am elevated

in the beginning
a word

in *my* beginning
a word
oh yes
oh yes

with the stroke
of the pen
upon paper
I elevate myself

this
is my story

not moving

what is the movement
of a motionless man

is he a drifting
in the sea

he has drawn attention
to himself
by standing still

is he afloat
among the stars

the act of no movement
is a shift
away from this world

is he suspended
like a bird

the more he stills
the more
he leaves us

is he a reflection
of the sun

what is the motion
of the man
who is not moving

forest I

I am the forest

I am
the river
and the trees

I do not start
I do not end
I
traverse myself
on paths well worn
and
fainter tracks

I am the predator —
hunter —
of my own forest floor
in water
in trees

and I am prey
vulnerable
to myself
as I quest and browse
all directions

through the forest
I am

into the grandeur

the resonance of raindrops —
falling
out of a cloud-grey sky —
reached him

drop by drop . . .

he raised his head
to let water touch
his face

to kiss his eyes

a gift of love
from above
to below

he spun around
through all degrees
the sky

the rain

forever right now
right
now

he released a breath
he did not know
he had been holding tight

his air
into the rain
sent out in offering
to the grandeur
that he felt
from deep inside
himself

aficionado

at the sounding
of the first note
she was lost

the interaction
of sound
and air
and self
undid her

before the second note
was struck
she had plunged forward —
headlong —
into the deep

a baby
awash in an amniotic space
surrounded with the promise
of richness

and she
a vast unfolding of *self*
with every exposed particle
of being
sensitized to receive

she waited
fully immersed
fully lost
entwined
in the ecstasy
of expectation

a breath (from the horizon)

the breath he took
inhaled air
sourced from the mists
on the horizon

he drew it in
in silence

thought to himself

    ah

the cords in his throat
tightened
and vibrated
as they must at the idea
and —
even in their own silence —
shaped the sound

    ah

the air that he inhaled —
from the purity
of the horizon
vast —
was a shape like

    ah

    ah

    ah ah ah

like a song

immense walk

she walked
in a blank solitude

across the white plains
of unmarked paper

from her mind
drew the features
of her land

> *green grass*
> *path pebbled*
>
> *trees*
> *away to mountains*

~

she walked on

across the white plains
of nothing
but white paper

from her mind
the yellow sands

rolling dunes
of solitude

footprints
in a single trail
behind her

sun shape and shadow
to come

~

while she walked
the white plains
of unetched paper

her feet wet
from a rising tide
of sea

from her mind

> *breath held*
> *shoal-fish surrounding*
>
> *anemone embrace*
>
> *coral bed*
>
> *lay down*
>
> *to sleep and dream*

~

she walked on
across a white plain
of blank paper

left her footprints
across the page

desert and the waiting sea

I
and the sky . . .

we are in
communion

sky watches over me
reaches down
to touch me
at the end
of day

at the end of time

the blue
and the gold

we are as one

and when the wind
hurls me —
playing —
right up into the air . . .

I am dust

I fall back
to myself
and dry
to the very earth itself

I do not change
I turn my shape
into a dune
to roll around
beneath my friend
the sky

~

be still

hush now

I will not harm you

no mud
will I let sully
your golden skin

take my shells –
my nacreous gift –
take all my flotsam

shh
shh

I will sweep high
on you

I will sweep low

shh
shh

I have a home
for every grain of you
that blows away
or washes
from your rolling dune

be still

hush now

and when I rage
I will rise to take you
in my water arms

piece by piece
and grain by grain by
crashing wave
tempest wave

that is when
I will claim you

but for now . . .

shh shh

be calm

roll around
beneath the sky

your friend

and when you roll
in the end
to where I am
you know
I
will be waiting

inside/out

he was locked *in*
to be kept
out

~

each day he walks
the boundary line
of his exclusion

and the guns
and the guards

the wires strung
keep him where he is

where he was

to keep him out

his dream —
daily now —
is remade

a ragged ragged
thing of shreds
draped against a fence
he dare not approach

and it would be funny —
if he allowed it —
almost amusing
to reflect that
where he had been he'd dreamed
of here

and the dream he dreamed then
was free

small

a guttering of softened light
beckoning
towards a warmth
that surely awaited him

now he is here —
truly here —
his dream is in a lock-down

now he is here
there is no *free*

only the cage

it was a dream

just a dream

and at night —
every night —
he strives
in all the ways he can
to release it

the deformity

his deformity
was a dangerous word
that contorted him
until he wrote it

that it flowed
into a poem
counted nothing

to see it on the page
was to know
a moment of peace
but
even then
renewed tension
had begun

it bent his mind
though he wrote
and wrote

the need
made him near crazy

he passed the days
in the light
of a window
a copy-paper ream
torn open

he
nearly spent

the sheets filled
with his derangement
like scribbled snow
scattered
to surround him

the fossil hunters expedition (part 1)

the school
of archeological literature
sent a team out
on a dig

an expedition

rumour had spread
that they had located
a fossil field
of significance

buried
beneath pages

the team was charged
to burrow down
through the years
with magnifiers
and tweezers —

an egyptologist too
(on loan
from cairo) —

through cliché
after cliché

their quest was to find
the first hardened specimen
of a metaphor

the search began
at an open door
into the past

that door

he should not
have imagined that door

he should not
have imagined
the handle

he shouldn't have seen —
through the eye
of his mind —
the turning of the handle
to *open*

he should not have heard
the latch give way
or the sound of hinges
in their first
creaking movement

shouldn't have stared
at the darkness revealed
or been
so
drawn towards it

we lost him
at the closure

none of us
could
conjure a key

that door was his
and no-one else
could follow

but
he *shouldn't* have

how we wished
he *hadn't*

why
did he imagine
that door

two sides of the door

the man who placed
his hand
to the door-knob
was confident . . .

quite *certain*

as he twisted
to convert the mechanism
from *closed*
to *open* he remained
determined

almost . . .

eager

.

.

.

so
how to describe
the sobering effect
of
an open space

it is difficult
for there is nothing there

nothing tangible

a mystery
that has to be
entered
before it can be solved

.

.

.

the man who closed the door
clung to the door-knob
for some time
after the latch had caught

snibbed

he felt a great
reluctance
to release it

for he knew
that then
he must turn around

and he was sure —
quite sure —
that he did not want
to do that

consumed by the poem (rare fruit)

she stepped
into the orchard
where the rays of the sun
fell over her
like a honeyed stream

a daze of light

flowers
full on the boughs
a bent invitation
seeking
with a touch
to pollinate her

fruit
strange fruit
everywhere
all around

the one she brushed
with a finger
shone
a glow
then came away
on her hand

fruit . . .

this strange
rare
fruit

while she held it
on the palm of a hand
consumed her

around the world

the world and I
are round
you know

we spin
each
in our own
peregrination

we
so like a ball
but
only I rebound
should I . . .

when
I fall

when I stumble

the world
turns on —
once in a while
to gaze at me

briefly —

then she spins away —
so sure —
upon her destined path

while I
rebound
resiliently

a right to equality (through a comprehension of parts)

she understood

the work
was a whole thing

more so
than segments and
portions

chapters
and stanzas

yet
as a reader
she found the imagery
of the complete work . . .

overwhelming

    so much

    so many

in her way
though
she felt
that she was —
perhaps —
the equal of the poem

of the poet

by focusing
on the small

reading
just a part
she could
comprehend

she understood the work
in segments
and
in that way
completely

she knew
it was a foolish notion
but she could not
help it

she felt as proud
of her parts
as the poet must have felt
of the whole

and
it was enough

brimming (he was)

he was
the squeaking sound
of the kitchen door
slowly
closing

the muffled footsteps
of young feet
climbing the stair
to his bedroom

his expectation
was the green
vista
of garden —
of vegetables —
growing in neat rows

and the trees
of the orchard
glimpsed
through the sheer curtains
of a kitchen window
that descended
to the height
of a small boy's eyes

his
was the darker gloom
of the tool shed
and the rough cording
of wood
stacked outside

his fingers claimed
the smoke
and the curing ham
that filled
the abandoned laundry

converted
into a smoke house
by his grandfather

and —
at the furthest back
of the land —
he
was the responsibility
for feeding the chickens

the eggs
filling an enamelled pail
to the brim

the bedroom

I could tell you
about the boy
I was

in my bed
about a hundred years
ago

sometime
last century
at least

my ceiling
was pine boards
with faces

knothole eyes

knot hole
nose

this one
is a polar bear

that one
is my uncle

if I squint my eyes
I see them all
descending

.

.

.

whose
is that labrador

did he belong
to a boy
like me . . .

one time —
in a fever dream —
I saw a spaceship
at the end of my bed

an alien

the idea

it came
out of a dream

it came
like lightning

even the *perhaps*
of rumbling thunder
was not
before

it wasn't there
it wasn't
anywhere at all

until
it was

the carving

the shape
emerges slowly
a little
at a time

unusual
with its formed curves
and curlicues

a cosmic representation of
a sway
shimmered by a breeze
kissing a path
across a still pond

never seen
never carved before

one of a kind

except for . . .

a resonance

held faintly
by air
carried up
from the deep below

and what of that

so what
if the echo
was at home in a curl
shaped
out of a new desire

this
is romance
and the carving
is still young

ontol-echo

a touch
that pushed
gently

released a sound
into the quiet air . . .

an exhalation

adrift

on its own path

until
it kissed the wall
before it —
sent an echo back —
then drifted off
again

and the echo
reverberated softly
around the gentle touch
it found

whispered
faint

more faintly

    I
    am

I

am

I

am

he is not the same

he felt _him_
as a kind
of inner pressure

like a knot

a hard ball
of something that
needed

a need that grew

left no room
for peace

     agitation

     pushing

     restlessness

_he_ grew
inside
until _he_ felt bigger
than he was

until he
was pushed aside
and squeezed
while _he_ broke out

and then . . .

he was there
standing beside

and _he_ was there —
beside —
as well

each looked

each saw
no resemblance
at all

turned
and moved
away

see that

did you see *that*

no
how could you

did you see
that one there then

no
you could not

it isn't fair
to ask you

it isn't right

how could you
see that

when it wasn't there

or
over there

it wasn't
right behind you

until I thought it
so

captured inner

from a distance
his eye catches
what seems
an attractive light

an understated sense
of *gleam*

closer
words like
radiance
come into his mind

warmth

closer again
until
his nose is almost
touching
the canvas

his eyes studying
the mountain ridge —
in miniature —
of a mix of colours
that still —
even at this small distance —
somehow
mesmerize
with their vibrancy

they reverberate positive
temperature
so that he can feel it
even though

even though

it is just
a picture

the new poem

it was an old thing

> *rust carbuncled*
>
> *corrosion scabbed*
>
> *derelict*

but he took it in

> *sand blasted*
>
> *abraded*
>
> *subjected to pressure*
>
> *smooth into rough*

and

> *rough*
> *into smooth*

he toiled

> *more pressure*
> *to make a mark*
>
> *more pressure*
> *to blast his name*

muttering and muttering
to powder-coat this new
fragile thing

mutter mutter
say the words aloud
until they're strong
and it is new

formed

then
a bath

    dip
    dip
    into chromium

    dip again

it is only a decorative coating
but the shape
the structure
has transformed
from what it was
dirty
rusted

until
now it shines
it gleams

reflects
a mirror
for his soul

it is new
and it is beautiful
again

to the end

came a day
for writing

pen in her hand
and with paper
she wrote
herself

the little things

> *the love affair*
>
> *the breaking*
>
> *the things that made her small*
>
> *the morals she aspired to*
>
> *the discovery that losses*
>
> *and joys*
>
> *are the stuff*
>
> *that is life itself*

she poured her being
into the words

they grew

she
diminished

and at the end . . .

at the
in conclusion
there was nothing left —
of that life —
to say

~

came a day
for reading

empty heart
and beaten
she took a page
and read

as she read
her eyes
glittered where they
caught the light

she came to feel
that she knew the plot
and the next thing
to be revealed . . .

ahead of the page

she paced the room
as she pored
declaiming aloud

      words

      sentences

      whole paragraphs

and when she reached
conclusion . . .

the part that *should* have read
the end . . .

there was nothing there

no word was written
for *she*
had just
begun

a choir of whispers

in every corner of the room
a man stood

his face turned in
to the angle
of his walls

they each
spoke towards the wall —
hardly a sound above
suggestion —

first one
then another
until the end

     I am a lonely soul

said one

     there is an empty place
     in my heart

followed the next

the voices rose
even in their softness
caught by an acoustic trick

     moving air
     reverberation
     amplification

to roll
echoing faintly
around the higher reaches

Frank Prem

will you search
for me

asked the third voice

I will be waiting
always

as each whisper rose
from its own corner
they blended
blurred
into a gentle
rhythmic chorale
of longing
refrained

transforming

it was only a poem
a small thing really
that told the tale
of a frog

of a pond

and its water lily

gradual change
and transformation

she read it
quickly —
at first —
but slowing

the words
turned into images
watery situations
that her mind
translated
into moving pictures

a poetic cinema

she was aware
that she was reading

that this poem
was a tale
a story
offered up by a poet
she had never met

but the words
spoke
to her

somehow engaged her
line by line

word by word

she found a
rightness
in it

that it fit her
somehow . . .

exactly

at last
she finished her reading
with a soft sigh

it was a wonderful poem
and somehow
she felt
it had changed her

still
the remainder of the day beckoned
there were other tasks
to attend

she croaked —
once —
and hopped away

that became him

his friend
said

>   *it is the beret*
>   *F_*

>   *when I see the beret*
>   *I see you*

>   *when I see* any *beret*
>   *it is you I call to mind*

he considered . . .

yes
it was true
the beret and *F_*
could be considered
as one

for he would not be seen
without it —
jaunty
in its place —
upon his head

yet
he cannot help
but remember
there was a time
when a beret
was the idea
of *other* people only

his first beret
was a stranger —
a gift —
and it was *she*
who was a special part
of the creature who knew himself
as $F\_$
but over time . . .

she has gone
the beret
has remained

until now
it is *man plus beret*
that equals the sum
of $F\_$

without it
he is simply
not

real writing

as he read
he hardly noticed
the changes

paragraph by paragraph . . .

he became
more
as he read the lines

and felt
a flow
from himself
onto the page

and he felt
a flow —
back —
from the page

he could not
put it down

it *was*

he could not
let it go

he grew

> *with every word*
> *that he became*
>
> *and towards the bottom*
> *of the last page*
>
> *and towards the final stop*
> *at the very end*

he said

    this is me
    this is mine
    and this
    is what
    I am

    whose is the name
    that held the pen

    what right
    did that name have
    to wield the quill
    and the nib
    of me

in a rage
he rummaged through
the cupboard
beneath the stair

in his rage
he sought the shell
that fit the gun

an aspiration beyond ochre in a cave

he sat
outside the light
made by the fire

cast his eyes
into the shadows
of the night

there . . .

>   *the shape of trees*
>   *in black*
>   *a hint of green*

and over there . . .

>   *shadow*
>   *light*
>   *the boulders that he knew*
>   *as* honeyed
>   *under the day*

above him

>   *the stars spread*
>   *light points*
>   *in changing patterns*
>
>   *the moon*
>   *who came and went*
>   *to laws her own*

some part of him
knew
that this was beauty

that the night brought a mood
and a temper
that was its own

he would speak of it —
would sing —
had he the words

he watched
in holy silence
alone

a warm pride

an unconscious thing

as she reads —
intently —
the brow of her forehead
furrowed . . .

ridged

reflecting her attention
to the words . . .

her focus
on the extraction
and comprehension
of images

and when she *saw* —
understood
the idea
in what she had read —

her face smoothed

lightened

and a look of joy
emerged

it didn't happen
always
or often

but when she *saw*
she felt
warm

the conductor

he takes the reading of a book
seriously

it is not *always*
akin to a religious
experience
but
he *wishes* that it was

the times when words
on the page
seem trite
repetitive
derivative . . .

all very poor experiences
but
when the words
dance
the lines speak
and then . . .

then he finds
he is a kind of conductor

using a pointed finger
as baton

his mental reading
rises . . .

falls

swirls in a torrent
of words

beautiful
to declaim aloud —
like a renaissance bard —
in his mind

fresh

there are passages here —
in the book she holds —
that she has read
three times
before

she knows them well
beginning to end
and
in the middle

she knows them all

yet here
today —
only three pages in —
she is engaging
with the heroine

worryings
about the adventures
in store

perhaps
suspension from the cliff . . .

this time
perhaps she will not recover
to save them all

knowing the end . . .

    ha!

well what of that

it doesn't change the journey
when she has become involved
anew
and who would not
be that unfinished
boy/girl/man/woman
on the way
to evolving into
the hero

she knows the end —
yes —
but she is discovering
the *now*
all fresh and new

she was different
when she read it before
and so
even if the end
is the same still
the story
has grown

saddle up

holding the pen
in his hand —
not yet having ventured
a single mark —
the writer paused

mid-thought
he was shivered
by a feeling . . .

as though
he were being watched

paranoia
perhaps
but the impulse
to glance behind
was irresistible
though fruitless

he began a line
tense
but alert to his creative impulse

and as the words flowed
more freely
he felt again the presence
riding *with* him now
anticipating his ideas
before they had been fully exposed
from the suggestive shapes
of his initial loops
and flourishes

it was benign

it was
encouraging . . .

eager

the more he sensed it
the more urgently
he wrote

galloping

and *oh*
the joy he felt
both his own
and that of another
unseen

chapter . . .

verse . . .

he wrote to exhaustion
finally
throwing down the pen

enough!

and gradually
he became aware
that he was —
again —
alone

the presence withdrawn
at the conclusion
of the work

weary weary
but so productive
to feel the desire —
the *need* —
for the story
that came from somewhere
outside himself

tomorrow
they would saddle up
and write
and read
once more

necessary preparations

remembering the last time
she resolved
on this occasion
to be prepared

beside her
she had laid out
a range of possible requirements

> *bow and quiver*
> *filled with arrows*
>
> *snorkel and mask*
>
> *an evening suit*
> *with bow tie*
>
> *hiking boots*
>
> *fishing line and a lunch-box*
> *containing three cheese*
> *and lettuce*
> *sandwiches*
>
> *drinking glass*
> *filled with water*
>
> *chain mail vest*

laying them down
within easy reach
she surveyed the assortment
nodded thoughtfully
to herself

> *yes*

they may not meet *every* possibility
but she felt
a little better prepared
for what may come

finally
she placed a large —
hand-drawn —
sign
penned in a red
permanent marker pen

    gone reading

being

he has written the line
but it doesn't read
right

he has read it now
three times

each reading
is *a near thing*

each rewrite
is *so close*

and he wonders
if the difference
between *a good thing*
and *a great thing*
is a matter of

> *heart*
>
> *of will*
>
> *of commitment*

his best work
flows from a wild abandon
but —
with this piece —
he has been *trying*
to write
trying
to read

perhaps . . .

perhaps it is his role now
to abandon
himself

perhaps
he has to stop
being *the writer*
the reader

to create the living work —
perhaps —
he needs to
be

writing certain senses

her vision
has taken the form
of a flower

she is writing it
delicately

> *the green of the stem*
> *the arc*
> *the infinitesima*
> *that is the point*
> *of the thorn*

momentarily
she comes to a halt
lost
within her narrative

closing her eyes
she casts her vision
inwardly
to recapture her sense
of the flower

when the bloom
is held —
clear again —
in her mind

she continues

> *petals*
> *stamen*
> *colour*
> *fragrance*

oh
the fragrance . . .

again she pauses
casting about inside herself
not for vision
but for aroma

the sense of it

> *sudden*
> *carried in*
> *on a soft breeze*
> *and halting conversations*
> *one*
> *after another*
> *as it proceeds through the room*

yes

she inhales deeply
seeking it

but no

reluctantly
she puts the pen down
on the desk

drastic measures
require her presence
immediately
outside in the garden
of roses

all included

to commence
he wrote his desk
and then the room . . .

his den

onto the page
went the window
the garden
the parkland
trees shrubs
a small dog

all of them

he incorporated the house
starting from the basement
rising to the attic
the chimneys

a line of pigeons
astride a ridge
running along the centre
of the roof

his street
the road
the houses
the neighbours
all of them
all of them
inserted
into the story

all that he could think of
all that he could imagine
he wrote

at last
when it seemed
he had included
the whole of the world . . .

he wrote his wife
his children

and then he was done

with a tear
running from a corner
of his eye
he looked around

saw nothing

seeing the flower

see that flower

the gardener pointed

it is there
it is growing
it is good

it is there
that I planted it

it is good
because I enriched the soil
for it to flourish

and now
you can see
that it has grown
very well indeed

I watered it
so the shoots could rise
and the buds could form

with my efforts
I have made
a very fine flower

~

I see the flower
yes

the second man responded

I see the flower

it is beautiful

here

where did I
come from

the voice resounded
an echo
in an empty room

how did I get here

what am I

hello

hello

~

it is not always easy —
she finds —
to write her thoughts
fully formed

sometimes
there is a start . . .

a beginning
but
a few lines in
she can't quite think
which direction
the new work
should take

~

is anyone there

I am frightened

hello

please

~

there are occasions

when she simply can't
think it through

when she regrets
having started
so falsely

paper in the bin

headache

despondence

today though . . .

today she believes
she knows

she puts pen to paper
and re-commences
what she had attempted
previously

~

hello

is anyone there

I
am here

for the unsuspecting

look out!

there are bullets in the air

there are bombs

everywhere he turns
every page
is filled with danger

> *oh!*
> *duck your head*
> *duck your head*

that was a close one

this book
is a war zone

he can't put it down
can't walk away
until the end

he can see
through the eyes
of the words
of the author
on paper

he can taste
the dirt in his mouth
from the shell-burst
that made his tea
go cold
before he drank it

this is so real
the next whistling missile
could end it

look out!
take care with that page
when you turn it over

there could be trouble

there are bullets
everywhere
and bombs primed

for the unsuspecting
reader

    don't forget
    to drink
    your cup of tea

changing the story

sit down!

behave!

do you forget
who wrote you

I have no intention
of allowing you
to run around
in any way you choose

this story you are telling
comes from *me*
you will recall

but I look at you —
written yesterday —
and do not recognize
the colours that you wear

I look at you —
this morning's words —
and find the story
that *I* thought
you have changed

who told you
that you may alter . . .

who
gave permission
to shuffle
all of my thoughts around . . .

I would put a line through
I would delete you
but . . .

I find I am
a little bit
engaged

interested

to find out
what you will say
when next I turn my back . . .

when next *I* pour
more
of what I think
and what I saw today
what I am

how will you change the story
of me

potter

there

she has sat
at the wheel
commenced it turning
by her foot
working the pedal
to get up the necessary speed

her material
is a poor ingredient
used many times before

garnered
from here and there

worn stuff
wetted into a slurry
that rides the wheel
round and round

she makes singing sounds
to give a tune
to work with . . .

to meditate into

to begin to shape

and the slurry
becomes
beneath her touch

she raises it
from mass
into a form

singing
humming
shaping

until it is *there*

her creation

whole
but soft and weak

a delicate thing
to her eye

quick

careful

into the kiln now

these words
are not yet
set in place

they must pass
through fire

then glaze

and fire
again

they are no longer
what they once were
no

they are
beautiful

down

was it a slip
into the water . . .

    a push
    a dive

    a fall

down here
it doesn't matter

the *why*
is up above

the *when*
is left behind

the *who*
she cannot recall

this is *here*
there is only
down

only
a ray of sunlight
slicing
to *forever*

through the sparkle
of the water
into deepest blue

    swim
    stroke
    paddle

she will follow

a fisher of storms

at the prow
he stands

waiting

above the swirl
and turmoil

the movement
is a maelstrom

the whirlpool
is a shoal

~

down
in the teeming
he *senses* one . . .

it is
the one he desires
to know

he dives

casts his heart in
before him
held sharp and pointed
like the spear
of his intention

deep
deep down his diving

and far
far away below

mind on the prize

one . . .

the only one
in that entirety of teeming

a thrust
sharp
of his spear point

what has he caught
he cannot know
until he rises

he can look then
at his prize

back on board
and sailing
again

across smooth oceans

ever on
ever on
to distant storms

the third lifetime

he has spent a lifetime
learning

knowing

another lifetime

forgetting . . .

everything

the third
was time spent
in thinking

doing

and in the end
he died

awake

aware

as free as suns

she wrote
in short lines

crisp
clear
sharp

unadventurous —
it is true —
but
sufficient
for her purpose

stanzas
of briskly expressed
words

black
onto the white

satisfied
she *flick*
flicked
a lighter
until it caught
and held a flame

the paper
of course
burned readily

but each word
was left
to hover
exposed
in the air

with all the paper gone —
and after the flame —
they gleamed
golden

then began
to swirl
fire and light

dazzling as suns

it was only
for a moment
and the blindness was
after all
temporary

a small price
to see her poem
burned free

the freedom of storms

the storm
was nearing

gusts of wind-song
sounded
then softened

and silenced

while —
higher up —
the sky was a-scud
with the movement
of billows
and frowns

he removed all his clothes —
except his red jockey underwear —
and wandered outside
into the heart
of a still moment

lay down on his back
in the centre
of a small patch
of lawn

and waited

there had been heat
this day
and the breeze —
at first —
was tepid and slow

barely enough to ruffle

but a sharp lick
saw goose-bumps rise

harbinger
of the cold front

the chill held him
to a shiver
but he almost leapt
into air
as a first
fat droplet
struck his chest

before an irregular pattering
caused a kind of prone
skeleton dance
where cold kissed warm

then —
finally —
it grew serious

rain falling steadily

wind crying a cold
fierce lament

and he —
thoroughly soaked now —
releasing his awareness
to rise up
into the weather

so constant —
the deluge and the buffeting —
he found it hard to breathe
as he was beaten
and beaten again
all over

he wanted to laugh
at the thoroughness
of his purging

but a small thing —
inside —
restrained him
with a whisper

you're going to drown yourself
you bloody
bloody
fool

surprising the Appreciation Society

well
what I try to do
is to surprise
you

you are the
who
and you are the
why
for me

she is speaking
giving a little talk
to the Appreciation Society

but
when I consider
the what
and the how
that might allow me
to craft your surprise . . .

I am
at a loss

for I do not know you
and likely
never will

the hall
is completely silent

there is no
shushering movement
of squirmed discomfort
or late arrival

no coughing
to drown out
the speaker's key points

> and so I find
> that I must write
> in a way
> that lets my story
> tell itself
> while I influence –
> only marginally –
> the direction and the fluency
> but leave substance
> to its own device
>
> when my work is done
> the piece
> is written
> and I can look at it
> as though new

the audience
attends closely
as she approaches
a finale

> and I find
> that it is I
> myself
> who is the first
> to be surprised
>
> and if it surprises
> even me
> who wrote it
> then surely . . .
>
> surely
> it will also
> surprise you
>
> thank you

in one clean movement
the audience
rose
from his seat

applauded politely

then turned and —
stumbling slightly —
made his way out of the hall
and into the adjoining
kitchenette
and small reception room

for a cup of tea and —
amazingly —
a piece of lamington sponge cake
still in the packet

unopened

only here, only now

I have no imagination

I just wait —
right here —
to see what happens next

one plus one
is not an idea

it only happens
if I am holding *two*
in my hands

don't speak to me
about tomorrow
and
don't ask me
to understand something
you are afraid of
or
looking forward to

I can't experience
your anticipation

but
I'll tell you what . . .

let's wait and see
what happens

you know
someone pointed me
towards a picture
once
but all I saw
was paint

sloppy

I am living *here*
and now

you
are alive
only
if I can touch you

I don't know
what's going to happen
but . . .

I can't imagine
any change

Frank Prem

to measure the sweet spot

he craved a theodolite . . .

a *tacheometer*

to measure
and to keep up
with shifting ground

> *surveyor of the heart*
> *please measure the distance*
> *from here*
> *to happiness*
>
> *is it near*
>
> *is it far*
>
> *is the happy space enclosed —*
> *like a battle-axe piece of feeling —*
> *lost in a sea*
> *of empty acreage*

if he used an alidade
to figure all the angles
he might find . . .

> *there*
>
> *there is a place*
>
> *it's just around*
> *the corner*

maybe
if he steps out
the correct number
of paces . . .

in the cupboard beside the sink

oh oh
but when I was a child —
just a small wee fellow —
it was there

in the cupboard
beside the sink
within the kitchen
of that first house
my family ever owned

it was there . . .

where they kept
the flour bags

a nest
of sorts
for the very small creature
that was me

my
hiding place
where I could whisper
live imaginings

where I could listen
to everything
magnified
from safety

where the rays
that angled in . . .

that *almost*
angled in
were enough
to light my world

how did that happen

it was such a . . .

it was so very small

but
I remember
an entire world

jungle rescue

I can show you
a photograph
of the path . . .

dirt worn
and barely wide enough
for one

kept clear
only by the application
of a machete slash
and perhaps
the poking of a purely defensive
pointed stick

it is a trail that runs
by winding route
from the entry hall
through what was
once
a formal lounge

the boxes —
higgle-thrown —
rise high
in this feral
residential jungle land

no one alive can know
what they might have held
once
maybe that one
there
was a pizza

cockroach supreme I think

a pair of size eleven sandshoes
resided —
before the mice —
in that one

and here
was something
wet
that ate right through
a cardboard corner
and then the carpet
that might have been
a floral
once

tendrils —
supporting sundry wildlife
and spiders —
hang
from a cornice
and from the lightbulb

drooping grey
and swung
by a fortuitous
upper stratospheric breeze
they have joined confections

piled high
in all points
but for one —
forearm wiped
and clean stripe-smeared —
managed space
at a corner
of the kitchen table

sized right for one
if
she is small enough

a rodent
is beating its *tom-toms* well —
very well —
to sound the warning
from a lookout post
located high
among the peaks of mountains

Mount Pan-higher
Mount Dish-more

the rat
has seen me —
in occasional glimpses
of filtered light —
as I move between the refuse
and the discards

the shopping-bags of dirty plastic
and the swamp traps
poorly camouflaged by tricks
played out in shadows

armed only with my powerful disgust
and a sword
that I have named
Most Reluctant

I am coming in
to rescue and retrieve
a poor
lost
mountain climbing
residential-jungle dwelling
failure

who calls this midden
home

the astronomer

he can ride the sighting
from his telescope
to the dying heart
of *betelgeuse*
in *orion*

describe the horseshoe shape
of one particular
in a nebula

tell about
the galaxies —
so very many galaxies —
away beyond
the milky way

at night
his glance at the sky
knows a shooting star
to be a meteor

the ups and downs
the dips
and mountains
of the craters
that pock the moon

but
when he steps
inside his house . . .

when work is done

the world that he touches
is a stranger

he cannot see
the corded lines
of accumulating dust motes
edging the walls
of his hallway
doesn't realise
that his bed
has not been made today . . .

or yesterday
or . .

whenever

there is no food
on the fridge shelf
but
he thinks he recalls
a sandwich . . .

maybe
at lunchtime

all he knows
for sure
is the mental guide —
well worn —
to the cupboard
that holds his whisky
and a cut-glass tumbler

there is no ice

again

but the whisky bites him
hard enough
to forget that
on the rocks
was once the way
he liked it best and
anyway . . .

and anyway

soon enough
he will fall to bed

go to sleep

until his sky rises again
and he can sit astride
his saddle —
one eye to the viewfinder —
and ride the glance
of his telescope

to look deep
this time
at *alpha a*

and maybe —
if he's lucky —
alpha b

haven

building walls
is *not*
an art-form

they are made
from crude things

> *bricks*
> *rocks*
> *rubble*

it just depends
on what you are thinking

he has thought
twin rows of *rock*

has filled the rows
with large barrowloads
of rubble

> *foundations*
> *need to be strong*
> *don't you see*

he has thought
bricks

thought them
from clay

from straw
and from water

he has thought them *stronger*
with white lime
and cow shit

then pictured them
laid down —
row
upon row —
growing tall

with perfect corners
at ninety degrees

>   *one*
>   *two*
>   *three*
>   *four*

no need
for windows
and
no need for doors

there will not be any
come-and-go
here

this is a room
of his own

no *familiars*
no *strangers*

no
I was just passing by
thought I would call . . .

he can think up
the walls
in a moment

he can think them away
if he wants

this is a haven

refuge
and
retreat

and no-one
can reach him
in here
at all

I on solid ground

there is a storm
raging
across the heavens

I see the dark
destructive clouds
gather . . .

swarm and rumble

wind gusts
with the lash of driven rain

I feel the cut

I wear the blows

and still I stand

I
on the temple
of my home

I stand
inside my doors —
no room for storms

rage

rage

rage *you*
loudly
amongst the night

in darkness
I
am holding
to a flame
that shows me clear

who am I
and *why* am I

I can stand
against terrors —
flashed white on black —
across the heavens

for here —
on solid ground —
am I

the purpose (of the St Nemom machine)

it was
a queer contraption . . .

clear sides

a box of sorts

nothing within
but a kind of
vortex machinery
spinning incessantly
in a direction that —
when looked at closely —
appeared to be
backward

from an open-funnel arrangement
came a strange sound . . .

oddly attractive
but seeming somehow sad
and melancholy

creating the sensation
of a tang
on the tip of the tongue

like the sharp and slightly fruity
taste
of a sunny day
in a distant
young springtime

and the sound —
the song —
also seemed
backward

I asked the man
what he was doing

what his machine
was meant to achieve

> *do you*
> *have time*

> *do you have*
> *enough time*
> *sir?*

> *I do not*

he said

> *this machine*
> *the St Nemom machine*
> *is a storage unit*
> *for stray moments*

> *consider*
> *all the wasted time*
> *that washes around us . . .*

> *around the world*

> *so very much of it*

> *the St Nemom*
> *draws it in*

> *captures and contains it*

> *and sir*
> *when I judge*
> *it is enough*

> *why then . . .*

then

> *the future*
> *will be mine*

Frank Prem

to achieve silence

the rhythmic clang
of a hammer striking

    identify
    classify
    dismiss

the hum of a refrigerator
with motor engaged

    identify
    classify
    dismiss

the quiet chortle of a magpie
smugly self-amused

    identify
    classify
    dismiss

a rustle of clothing in the corridor
just out of sight

    identify
    classify
    dismiss

a cicada call
shrill but vague in the distance

    identify
    classify
    dismiss

the imagined whir of a single thought
colliding with another

> *identify*
> *classify*
> *dismiss*

a mimicry of insect chirrups and calls
ever-present inside her head

> *identify*
> *classify*
> *dismiss*

> *dismiss*

> *dismiss*

just finishing up now

the sheet is painted

the detail drawn

    here . . .

the house
where she grew up

mama at the roses
papa out the back
planting veg

    there . . .

the shady tree
with the marking
of birch-swept rooms
all around it

a tiny cup in the space
for a fine serving
of little-girl tea

the fence
she leant against
to receive a first —
fresh —
kiss

can you see the outline
of her sweetheart beau

    in a mirror . . .

there he is again
just after she said goodbye

young sadness
in that frame

and in the middle . . .

large at the start
then

fading . . .

the path she trod

the road she took
when she went away
for good

although she is —
really —
still
quite present

do you see . . .

that is the easel

and *there*
the paints

the brush seems still wet
and heavy
from the last scene
that
she is finishing up
just now

story read: story see

head down
book open
I read a page
that tells me . . .

> *information*
> *incident*
> *time and date and setting*
>
> *everything that happened*
> *everything there was*
> *to see*

head down
book open
I read

but
when I pause . . .

raise my eyes
above the page

I gaze far away

until I can look
inside the words
that run across
and down
the pages

the adventure starts

the story lives

changed a little . . .

just
a little bit
by me

a good write

she begins to read

    around the words

    inside the sentence

    past the paragraph

    beyond the page

she begins
to see

there

she could only do this
in pencil

graphite
or grey

    hb
    2b

    3h

she doesn't care

monochrome
by grey-lead

shades
that turn to
shapes
that turn to scenes
as the page becomes
a depth
and a diversity

    did that car
    just move
    on the roadway

    did the tree sway
    a little

    is that dog there
    barking
    with a tail wag

    someone
    concealed behind a shrub

the sound of a giggle
perhaps
a game

who gets to play . . .

she doesn't know —
not yet —
she is still shading

she is still shaping

she is still growing
this grey scene
until it is alive

without colour
but alive

and *there*

she has left
a small impression

a little patch
of *minus* space
not touched
by artist pencil

it remains
available

and in a moment
she will be there . . .

in just
another moment . . .

there

she will be

reflected into a corner

the mirror is watching
from a corner
of the room

I can see
reflections
but the mirror sees
what is *real*
then turns it back to me

opposite is *same*
inverted

the image matches me . . .

my movements

> *I dash right*
> *it dashes left*
>
> *the same*

I am confused

am I *reflected*

is it *me* in *there*

which of us is *real*

do *my* feelings count
at all

and does my image
also *feel*

where does it *go*
when I am not watching

I can't see it
from my corner

compartments

in his mind . . .

compartments

this one
here
holds the things
he knows

the next one
all his certainties

a third
the things
that he can do

one over there
is for memories
with ghosts resident
alongside

sometimes exchanging entrances

further on
we have his dream spaces

> *nighttime*
> *daytime*
> *reverie*

it is these
that he escapes to
when the other
compartment doors
begin
to make
their noise

bored

it started
gradually

a creeping sense
of non
involvement

things happened around her —
activated responses
and reactions —
but were in a way
beside
her

at some point
she became aware
that it was
a *buzz*

everything
a *buzz*
slowly filling her mind

she navigated
on auto-pilot
connecting with *this*
swerving from *that*

but without
herself
which was engaged
passively
by the *buzz*

over time
she seemed to become
smaller

further away

outside
of herself
began to ignore her

to non-involve
her
while *she*
failed to notice

smaller

she could not be sure
if she had lost something
or not but
as she shrank
away
she noticed
with almost
curiosity
the fall of one
slow rolling
tear

crossroads to new day

this one runs
directly
to the far off Never

dim your light

close your eyes
so they can adjust
then look

you can see that its colour
is ebony

that one there
is blocked and caved
and broken

I cannot say
what trouble might lie
beyond

behind us . . .

you know there is nothing
behind us
for long miles

nothing
but nighttime

that is where we live

where we have always
lived

the fourth way runs down

I think it could go
right to hell

no one
has returned
from that road
ever

so
you must
take the straight way

ahead
to that black horizon

if you go far enough
and
if you last
so long . . .

if you do not mistake
the darkness
for your death

there is a place I have heard
when the whispers
carry long
in the tunnels

a place
where the black
does not reach out
to kiss everything

what I have heard —
once or twice —
is that they call that place
new day

dream alive

a dream

a long unending dream
of leaves
twisting as they rise

of sun
shining brightness

nights that are warm

a yellow
smile . . .

a flower

a dream dreamed on
and dreamed on
like time locked
in a cell with no keys
and
without a door

a first touch
of water
to move through the darkness

a small touch
of water
to wake from slumber
the seed

send *down*
your white shoots

send *up*
your green

wake up
wake up

wake up
from your dreaming

wake
into life

impressionism

in pastel
the idea of *bird*
taking flight

done by suggestion

here
this way of applying colour
will soon
be a vehicle
car
driving at pace
on the road

and another

these lines are the trigger
for a vision of *horse*
in mid-gallop

there he goes
to the back
of the paddock

there it goes
only dust
left behind

and *there* it is
hovering
just like *hawk* . . .

out to catch
the suspicion
that I
will now insert

the scurry
of *mouse*

dwelling with two

anchor your dwelling
in me . . .

I am strong

I can hold you
in this

my earth

let your cellar
delve
deep inside me

place your secrets
in the clay
below your floors

I will keep them
sacred

~

raise your roof
into the sky

build a stair —
climb —
that I might see you

up here the air
is clear

the sun will shine

dark clouds
roll to the distance —
no damage done —
and you . . .

uplifted
you may behold
the day

rejoice to breathe . . .

to reach
high into the atmosphere

reach up
reach out
to me

the map

the map said

> *down*

the map said

> *ten steps*

the map said

> *buried in the*
> *left-hand corner*
>
> *near to the wall*

the map said

> *you need a spade*
> *now*
> *for here*
> *be buried tr . . .*

treasure
trouble

there isn't much
to choose between them
just one extra letter in a word
when they're written down
on the page

one extra character
that might mean

> *hip hurrah*

but
trouble . . .

trouble lies
in the darkest places
trouble
sneaks around

~

from her bed
safe
in the room above
the kitchen

she contemplates new ideas
of risk
and of reward

until weariness
finally intrudes
to take her over
to lull the girl
to sleep

and into dreams
of
the heavy door

a black keyhole
to a massive lock

and of the night
that rules the reaches
beyond the first step
leading down

if that door
should open

tidal street

the tide roars
down my street

every truck
confirms the ebb

until it seems
it must be twice-washed

first *clean*
and then
away

but ever yet
it will rush again

a tsunami
retreating

until a distant sound —
from the granite bridge
that serves as buoy marker
down at the bottom
of the street —
informs

the warning-vane
of one *incoming*

a mile of build

a mile
of sound
expanding —
enlarging north and south
while all the time rising
rushing east —
toward the morning
and a coming day

I wait . . .

the sound flows over me

is
past

the sea —
a storm —
is waiting
for the next sound-wave
to ebb and wash
beyond
a traffic tide

his name

> you
> cannot know
> the weather

he said

> you live
> in houses
> huddled in rows for safety
>
> in concrete
>
> on tarmac
>
> you are in shock
> when a wet hand
> of water . . .
>
> of rain
> reaches down
> and slaps you
>
> as though
> you do not matter
>
> I . . .
>
> I know this storm

he said

> I know his name
> I watch him grow
> his temper swell
>
> I see him

the old man mused

as he approaches closer
crying out
that he has come
for me

I am alone

my shack is small
and it is filled with holes
through which he sends
his early breezes

I name him **tempest**

that
makes him howl

for no-one should know him
for what he is

but the name was whispered
in his song
on a day
when he took my home
and the whole
of my world
away

I name him
devastation
to make him shriek aloud
and cry

he named me
defiance

blew me
down
then whistled himself
away

yes
I know this storm

you . . .

huddle closer

it yet may be
you could stay
safe

the hermits of reading

she
has been wandering

lost
in the darkness
of a densely treed forest

lost
long enough
to doubt her reason . . .

her *purpose*
in entering these woods
at night

but
it was a desperation
that drove her
that drives her still

clutching *fiercely*
her sole possession
of any value
in both hands
held tight against her body

~

she stumbles
comes near to falling
but rights herself . . .

maintains her grip

all the time
she is casting about wildly
as though to penetrate
the dark
with one
correct
glance

and *there* . . .

there

she sees it

surely
there it is

a flicker —
a small flower —
of light

she is saved

her purpose
holds

staggering now
she proceeds by path
and by tree root
until
the way is clear

the hut of the hermit
stands before her

light
spreads wide
from a single lantern
seated on the sill
of a window

clustered around
as far as the edge
of the spill of this illumination . . .

her fellow seekers

arrayed —
each with his personal
most precious possession —

open
printed pages
held
to the light

lips move . . .

fingers touch the page . . .

but each holy word
is read
in reverent silence

to make it habitable

it was quite an enterprise

a truck arrived
filled with flat packs
deposited
one atop the other

he worked at a furious pace

> *opening*
> *checking contents*
> *assembling*

he was adept
for
in a short time
the cellar was assembled
and inserted

> *a floor*
>
> *the kitchen*
> *living*
> *lounge*
> *dining*
> *den*
> *bedroom bedroom bedroom*
> *bath and shower*
> *smallest room*
> *hallway*
> *front door*
> *back*
> *stairs down*
> *stairs up*
>
> *the attic*
>
> *the roof*

unpacked and assembled

complete

but . . .

lacking something . . .

some *element*

it was found —
of course —
in the last pack

a much smaller container
able to be carried
easily
by the man

he moved systematically
into and out of every room

in each he paused
set down the container
opened it and removed
a small quantity
of a delicate
something

he wandered the room

    nooks

    corners

and deposited a sprinkle
of fine substance
in each

then returned

gathered his container
and moved on to the next room

spending more time
in the cellar

more time
in the attic

when he was done
the container
was empty

the house
was filled

the memories
and familiarities
of a lived life
in place
to welcome a new owner
home

do-si-do (a weatherboard quadrille)

in the night
the houses danced
as their owners
lay deeply slumbering

> *formal*

> *elegant*

> *forward*
> *then return*

all along the asphalt
arrayed
to the *two/four* blink time
of patterns
splayed
by the pulsations
of sodium lighting
from the kerb

silent —
the dancers —
but for a creak
from a weathered board

the scrape of a red brick
dragged

gentle
gentle movements
to lull into serenity
the slumber of their sleepers

until . . .

a formal bow

a gentle curtsy

then back

each to their allotments
while darkness
remained

to settle back
to rest
onto the strong foundations
that waited

ready to release them
again
for another quadrille

neighbourhood watch

one eye —
slowly —
casts its gaze

venetians rise
to halfway

the boulevard
is under surveillance

a shutter —
on the other side —
opens
to watch the lawns
and sidewalk

up the road
on a corner block
two paths meet
at a crossing

unblinking glass
overlooks . . .

watches them both

roller blinds
wind up and release

wind up
and release

their coded calls
communicate

    all is calm

    all is quiet

the surveillance
goes on

old winter

how old you are
dread *winter?*

in the deep of white
you keep memories

cold and pale
and withered

I have touched them —
as I must —
but every time
there has been
a price

ever and ever
a price
that claimed from me
some *thing* I held
that was
warm

there is a chill
in you
old *winter*
that comes from ages
long ago

before I knew
the traps of seasons

before I understood
to treasure sunshine

I am coming
towards you
winter

I am grown old
now
too

though you take
my warm —
as though by right —
I hold
a kernel . . .

a single memory

of the second *springtime*

the *rejuvenation*

one memory
not to be ceded
into your keeping

it is the one
that will keep me hale

warm my heart

though you lay
your ice upon me

as you will

too far *out of it* to go to work

he woke up
early

didn't feel well

he called his workplace
to say

> *I feel strange*
>
> *really strange*
>
> *I feel*
> *out-of-it*
> *somehow*
>
> *I don't think*
> *that I can focus*
> *so I won't be coming in*
> *to work*
> *today*

from work
they told him

> *okay*
>
> *gee*
>
> *you sound*
> *a long long way*
> *away*
>
> *get better soon buddy*
> *because*
> *we need you*

he wandered —
scratching an itch —
still more than
half asleep

stumbled his way
into the kitchen

turned the kettle on
at the power-point

pulled the ring
on the roller blind . . .

released
and raised it

it was night
outside
but
it *ought* to be day

there were stars
embedded
into the black

no twinkling

he shook his head
slowly
turned back
to pour the coffee

stepped
across the kitchen
to the back door

the first thing he noticed . . .

no verandah

but
a hundred million
miles of *nothing*

heading down

heading up

heading
all around

made him feel like he was

up
side down
and
falling

maybe
upward

maybe out

the weatherboard cladding
beside his ear
creaked loudly

made him jump

alarmed

he looked at his hand —
trembling —
spilling hot drink
onto the floor

but the house . . .

the house felt
fine

old california bungalows
you can take them anywhere

they seem to last
forever

he wondered
what he should do . . .

then stepped —
quiet as he could —
across the bedroom

pulled the curtain
to one side —
just to make
quite sure —

said —
almost in a whisper —
he said

    honey

spoke a little louder

said

    honey . . .

    can you wake up

    I didn't go
    to work today

    and
    honey . . .

    I've got something
    to show you

    something
    that you
    really
    need to see

unfriended **by the walls**

it began when a door
required readjustment

swollen
down below

sticking to the floorboards

a physical thing
for intervention
or
perhaps a carpenter
to talk to . . .

someone
who might understand

the window's problems
were more clearly
psychological

transparently neurotic
but still
a form of psychic discomfort
surrounded
by blank stares

one by one
the foundation pieces
moved out
and then moved on

the outer walls
were weary . . .

a vacation might refresh

perhaps
a painting weekend . . .

somewhere
with a palette
of brighter shades

the kitchen
and the bedrooms
felt they could not bear
to hold up
when they'd been left —
teetering —
without support

~

fallen to the ground

de-shingled
and dishevelled

unfriended and alone

the roof
is now contemplating
entering a relationship
with a basement
which is little more
than a hole
in the ground

plugging

every so often
she would have to stir herself
because

the floors
would begin to thin
and the ceiling
to creep a little lower

and
the sound of rain
falling down

    away

would become
too much like
a waterfall

then
she would seize
her cloud-grey plugs
and load them into
the cloud-plugger

she would swim
around the bottom
of the world
looking for the holes
that must be infused

one by one

hour by hour

hole
after drizzling hole
she filled them

occasionally
there would be a new downpour
and she would have to
start again

but
she swam
and plugged
until
the levels stabilized

then she would
glide through the water
back
to her home
again

happy
just to *be*
until the next
cloudburst
when she would have to start
plugging again

before the world
rained itself completely
away

memories of bathing

he takes off
his shoes

socks
pants
and his shirt

naked is the way
to go forward
from here

he has tried
to use clothing
to cover himself over

to attempt the concealment
of what stands
self-condemned

but he is only
one man
whose shames
are just the small sins

of deeds he has done
and *ought-to's*
somehow forgotten

one foot
into the water
begins
dissolution

every hard resolve
he has committed himself to
melts
in this way

into the water
out of the shell

the old memories
that wash over him
are a forgiveness

breathing life into the garden

the exhalation of his breath
was like
a thin
grey
smoke

pallid

minute movements
of his lips
and great concentration
shaped directions

in the clear air
he saw a garden

in the exhaled mist
a row of flowers
white

behind them
he blew a façade
of the happy house
that he recalled

another breath
another exhalation
and detail placed

kneeling

kneeling on the white lawn

tending

a familiar shape —
the gardener —
who had once made the flowers
grow
in so many different colours

his breath caught suddenly

he coughed —
gently —
then turned away

calling a cockatoo

a piercing
two-fingers-in-your-mouth
whistle

repeated

emitted again

leaving ears ringing
but
no other result

he gazes —
a little forlorn —
at the upper reaches
of the mirabelle tree

whistles again

a plum falls

two

the whistle resounds

dejectedly
the boy turns away
wanders slowly
to the house
where he looks
accusingly . . .

resentfully

at his brother

    it's not working

    it won't work

    you <u>know</u> it won't work

his brother

smirks
but says nothing

in the tree
a snow-white cockatoo
snacking on the golden fruit
drops another plum
to the ground

experiencing
a momentary confusion

usually
the bird is a little more
sure-footed

the colour of light

he has spent a long time
trying to see . . .

> *what colour is the light*
> *today*

he isn't thinking
of refraction
or rainbow
but

> *what* light
> *is today*

something bright
and brilliant

yesterday
is already
a fainter shade

memories of youth
somehow hold
a rosy
pink-tinged
hue

the room he slept in —
then —
seems toned in the glow
of amber

that of his parents —
just next door —
is duller

sepia-hued
and empty

so *many* lights
all so different

how do they change . . .

does the colour
leach
with distance
or
is there perhaps
a compartment-shuffle
within the memory

so much time
spent in warm shades
then
move along
to cool

fade away
to end
in snowy speckles

he has spent a long time
trying to imprint
the colour of the light
today

the wind thief

she built her trap
from ground
up
into the air

baited it with vanes
in the shape
of a cross

released to spin
at the first touch
of the first
passing zephyr

> *around*
> *around*
>
> *the shaft*
> *thrums a chorus*
> *of crunch*
> *voiced*
> *by the action of its turning*

she watches —
adjusting angles

freeing movement —
until the pace of the spin
is right

then
she pours
her own wheat in

> *around and around*
> *the shaft*
> *thrums the song*
> *of the crunching of wheat*
> *and the turning*

the wind does not deign
to notice

what —
after all —
is a little less air
when it can blow through the sky
without concern

so she steals
from the breeze

enough puff
to turn

enough to crunch
and to grind her wheat
to flour

the glow in the table (heart and soul)

he found it
half buried
under some rubbish
at the back of a shed
that was the junk shop
for the town

old blackwood tables —
with extension leaves —
show up that way
from time to time

it was the work
of his heart —
when he got it back home —
to separate it
into its parts

  re-carpenter
  the legs and leaves

all handcrafted original pieces

  service the winder
  and its mechanism
  for extension

he took his time

sanded it back to smooth
but
keeping the old life within it
as a kind of
celebration

  oil coat to finish

his heart swelled

he had always understood
that to give your work
life
you had to put in
your own *soul*

and
as he opened up the polish
that
was where he'd placed
his mind

cloth in hand
he rubbed
while the blackwood ate up
the wax

and as he joined
with the rhythm of the rub
the wood
began to glow

dream, draw, home to bed

he drew a picture of a house

> *chimney*
> *red roof*
> *and windows*

in the picture
he drew himself
opening a door

~

he drew a picture
of a kitchen

pots
stove
and table

in the picture
he drew himself
stealing biscuits —
hot —
right off the tray

~

he drew a picture
of a hallway

> *flower pot*
> *umbrella stand*
> *grim faces*

he drew himself —
mid step —
climbing up the stairs

~

he drew a picture
of a bedroom

> *books*
> *wall posters*
> *model planes*

he drew himself
pulling up blankets
snuggling in the bed

going back to sleep

returning
to his dream

Bachelard Source Materials

Gaston Bachelard, French Philosopher lived from 27 June 1884 to 16 October 1962. The series of poems and poetry in this book has drawn inspiration from the following publications by Bachelard, translated into English.

Intuition of the Instant by Gaston Bachelard (1932) Eileen Rizo-Patron (Translator) Northwestern University Press, 2013

The New Scientific Spirit, by Gaston Bachelard (1934), A. Goldhammer (Translator) Beacon Pr; 1st Edition (1984)

The Psychoanalysis of Fire, by Gaston Bachelard (1938), A.C. Ross (Translator) (1964).

Lautréamont, Gaston Bachelard (1939), Robert S. Dupree (Author), James Hillman (Author), Dallas Institute Publications; Reprint Edition (2012)

Water and Dreams: An Essay on the Imagination of Matter by Gaston Bachelard (1942), Edith R. Farrell (Translator) (1983.

Air and Dreams: An Essay on the Imagination of Movement, by Gaston Bachelard (1943), Edith R. Farrell (Translator), Frederick Farrell (Translator) Dallas Institute Publication Dallas Institute Publications (1988)

Earth and Reveries of Will: An Essay on the Imagination of Matter by Gaston Bachelard (1943), Kenneth Haltman (Translator) Dallas Institute Publications (2002)

Earth and Reveries of Repose: An Essay on Images of Interiority by Gaston Bachelard (1948), Mary McAllester Jones (Translation), Dallas Institute Publications (2011)

Dialectic of Duration. Gaston Bachelard (1950), Mary McAllester Jones (Translator), Rowman & Littlefield Publishers; (2016)

The Poetics of Space by Gaston Bachelard (1958), Maria Jolas (Translator) Penguin Classics (1964).

The Poetics of Reverie, by Gaston Bachelard (1960), Daniel Russell (Translator) Beacon Press; New Ed Edition (1971)

The Flame of a Candle, by Gaston Bachelard, (1961), Joni Caldwell (Translator) Dallas Institute Publications (1988).

The Right to Dream by Gaston Bachelard (1970), J.A. Underwood

(Translator) Dallas Institute Publications (1988)

Fragments of a Poetics of Fire, by Gaston Bachelard, Kenneth Haltman (Translator), Dallas Institute Publications (1988)

On Poetic Imagination and Reverie, by Gaston Bachelard, Colette Gaudin (Translator) Spring Publications; (2014)

Author Information

Frank Prem has been a storytelling poet since his teenage years. He has been a psychiatric nurse through all of his professional career, which now exceeds forty years.

He has been published in magazines, online zines, and anthologies in Australia, and in a number of other countries, and has both performed and recorded his work as spoken word.

He lives with his wife in the beautiful township of Beechworth in North East Victoria, Australia.

Connect with Frank

Find Frank at his website www.FrankPrem.com, or through Social Media online at Facebook, X (Twitter), Instagram and YouTube.

Other Published Works

Free Verse Poetry

Small Town Kid (2018)
Devil In The Wind (2019)
The New Asylum (2019)
Herja, Devastation - With Cage Dunn (2019)
Walk Away Silver Heart (2020)
A Kiss for the Worthy (2020)
Rescue and Redemption (2020)
Pebbles to Poems (2020)
The Garden Black (2022)
A Specialist at The Recycled Heart (2022)
Ida: Searching for The Jazz Baby (2023)
From Volyn to Kherson (2023)
Alive Is What You Feel (2023)
White Whale (2024)
Pilgrim Volume 1 - Illustrated by Leanne Murphy (2024)
A Poetry Archive Volume 1 (2024)
A Poetry Archive Volume 2 (2024)
A Poetry Archive Volume 3 (2024)
A Poetry Archive Volume 3 (2024)

Picture Poetry/Spoken Image

Voices (In The Trash) (2020)
The Beechworth Bakery Bears (2021)
Sheep On The Somme (2021)
Waiting For Frank-Bear (2021)
A Lake Sambell Walk (2021)
A Few Places Near Home (2023)
The Cielonaut (2024)

What Readers Say

Small Town Kid

A modern-day minstrel. Highly recommended.
—A. F. (Australia)

Small Town Kid is a wonderful collection.
—S. T. (Australia)

Devil In The Wind

Trust me, this book will stay with you. Bravo!
—K. K. (USA)

Moving, beautiful, and terrible. I was left with a profound sense of respect, as well as a reminder that we should never take for granted every precious every moment of life.
—J. S. (South Africa)

The New Asylum

Words can't do justice to the emotional journey I travelled in (reading this collection).
—C. D. (Australia)

If I had to pick one book over the past year that has truly resonated with me, this would be it.
—K. B. (USA)

Walk Away Silver Heart

Instantly grips you by the throat in his step-by-step story of survival. Bravo!
—K. K. (USA)

Outstanding!
—B. T. (Australia)

A Kiss For The Worthy

A Celebration of Life Written in Thoughtful Bursts of Poetic Expression
—C M C (United States)

With every verse, I found myself reflecting about myself, my life, and the world.
—K

Rescue and Redemption

The passion of love in its many forms explored by one for another.
—J L (United States)

I've enjoyed every word, every breath. Every moment within the life of these stories.
—C D (Australia)

Sheep On The Somme

Museums and archivists take note~sell this in your gift shops, preserve it in your archives. Professors, teachers~share with your students.
—A R C (United States)

(This) book is a beautiful and graphic tribute to all those brave men and women who gave their lives for their countries between 1914 and 1918.
—R C (South Africa)

Ida: Searching for The Jazz Baby

I found myself deeply moved by the presentation of Ida's elusive, illusionary life.
—E G (United States)

He gives her a depth and vulnerability that the press didn't.
— A C (United Kingdom

The Garden Black

Prem creates verse that illuminates our world, its experiences and history.
—S C (United Kingdom)

Prem's poetry reminds that life is fragile and fleeting ... both harsh and beautiful.
—D G K (Canada)

A Few Places Near Home

The author has captured many beautiful images in this book, and is a wonderful photographer as well as a poet. This book would make a beautiful coffee table book filled with moving prose to make us ponder with gorgeous accompanying images.
—D K (Canada))

www.FrankPrem.com